THE PEPPER PARTY

Double Dare Disguise

By

JAY COOPER

Scholastic Inc.

SCHOLASTIC

For Rocky. And Ben.

ISBN 978-93-8982-330-1

First printing 2020
Book design by Nina Goffi
This reprint edition, August, 2023
Printed in India at Shiavm Offset Press, New Delhi

CHAPTER 1

"Good morning, San Pimento! It's gonna be a *super* day!" Megs Pepper yelled out her bedroom window to the whole neighborhood.

Her grumpy old neighbor Mr. Jenkins, who was taking out his trash, waved her off. "Ah, nuts!"

She closed the window with a smile. Every

day was special, but today was, well . . . super special!

Today was Comic Con Day!!!

It was well known that Megs Pepper was a fan of all things sporty. She loved baseball, basketball, soccer . . . even curling. She loved sports so much she'd even invented a whole new one: froosbetball (a combination of Frisbee and basketball). Her bedroom walls were lined with posters of her favorite teams and athletes.

But these were everyday heroes, and they only covered three of her four walls.

The fourth wall of Megs Pepper's room was devoted to a hero who was much more super than any of those . . . A REAL superhero, in fact! Megs Pepper looked up in wonder at the absolute best superhero of all time: Centaura!

Centaura's trademark power was turning into a centaur—a creature from Greek mythology who was half human, half horse—when danger was truly great. But unlike the centaurs in ancient myths, Centaura used her powers to fight modern-day crime! She had left her fabled island of Equinia and traveled to Girder City, where she lived under the not-so-secret identity

Centaur from Mythology

of Delores Duchess. Centaura never shied away from danger, and she used her uni-horn of power and her coat of invisibility to protect mankind from harm. Just like Megs, she always had a super positive attitude!

Megs had collected all of her comic books. She'd gone to see her most recent movie five times in the theater and owned almost the entire line of Centaura action figures. Megs loved Centaura so much that she'd even dyed her hair the exact shade of Centaura's purple mane.

But Megs had never had the chance to actually meet Centaura . . . UNTIL TODAY! It just so happened that Delores Duchess, Centaura herself, was going to make a rare appearance at the San Pimento Comic Con.

CENTAURA
UNI-HORN OF POWER!
BY THE POWER OF EQUINIA!!!
CENTAURA'S HIDDEN FORTRESS: THE TEMPLE OF TIME-OUT!

Her wall of Centaura posters was almost entirely covered except for one spot where purple paint poked through. By the end of the day, Megs would have met her hero, and she'd have a signed poster hanging there to prove it!

But Megs wasn't the only Pepper that was excited for Comic Con.

All the Peppers were getting ready for an awesome day at the convention.

Every year, Tee Pepper dressed up like one of her favorite TV characters for Comic Con. This year she had chosen Queen Celery, the villain from the show *Game of Musical Chairs*. Sure, Queen Celery was an evil schemer, but she schemed with style!

Ricky Pepper was also dressing up as his favorite character: Private Patriot, the leader of the Defenders of Justice Club from the best-selling comics and movies. Ricky admired the Private's sense of justice, but secretly, he mostly just had a giant crush on Plucky, Private Patriot's wisecracking teenage sidekick.

Scoochy Pepper had created her own character for Comic Con, a villain named Bad Baby. She'd even come up with an especially evil laugh to use when pranking unsuspecting heroes. Maria thought Scoochy's character could have real box office appeal, and had decided to become a super agent and represent her.

Annie wasn't dressed up at all. An aspiring reporter, Annie planned to film a segment at Comic Con for the San Pimento Network News. Her brother Beta Max normally acted as her cameraman, but he had his own plans

1. Megs Pepper (age 10) getting ready to meet her hero
2. Tee Pepper (mom) finding her inner queen
3. Beta Max Pepper (age 9) coveting a new video game system
4. Scoochy Pepper (age 2) practicing an evil laugh
5. Meemaw Pepper (ancient) looking for rare first edition

6. Sal Pepper (dad) polishing his chili trophy
7. Maria Pepper (age 9, plus 2 minutes) prepping her super agent pitch
8. Ricky Pepper (age 12) feeling patriotic
9. Annie Pepper (age 8) filming a news segment

today. The video game company Utari was unveiling its new Uplayit handheld game system at Comic Con. The Uplayit video game projected a holographic image of yourself playing the game as you played it! How cool was that?

Meemaw Pepper was going to do what she did every year: look for her father's comic book, *Presto Pepper's Magic Comix* #1! To say this comic was ultra rare was an understatement; there was only one copy left in the world. That was because Presto had hidden a stink bomb inside it that went off when you turned to the last page. Grossed-out mothers across the country had thrown them away as soon as they had come out, except for one last copy of the comic that had survived.

Sal Pepper was just excited to sell loads of his delicious chili to hundreds of hungry fans outside the convention. Nothing at Comic Con interested him as much as the trophy on his mantel. He'd won it for making the Nearly Best Chili at the annual San Pimento Chili Cook-Off. Every day he shined it with a special soft cloth, stared at it for at least fifteen minutes, and sighed happily.

CHAPTER 2

Tee Pepper called up the stairs, "Megs, honey, we're leaving for the convention now! I summon thee, peasant!" (She was already getting into character!)

"Coming, Mom!" Megs called back.

She looked in the mirror as she put on her official uni-horn medallion over her Centaura Fan Club T-shirt. She had done her own hair to look exactly like Centaura's mane.

"This is it," she said to herself. "The moment you've been waiting for!"

Megs had a special ticket that guaranteed her a signed photo with Centaura. She'd saved up her allowance for months to afford it. Nothing could possibly stop her now.

She smiled and picked up her lucky froosbetball. Then She spun it effortlessly on her finger. Then she passed it behind her back and threw it into her clothes hamper.

"Yep, this is going to be the best day ever," she said with a smile.

The behind-the-back-into-the-hamper shot was a move that Megs had done a thousand times before perfectly. The ball always bounced off the open lid and into the hamper, and then the lid closed on top.

But this time—shot number one thousand *and one*—the lid didn't close, and the froosbetball bounced out of the hamper.

It bounced onto Megs's bedroom floor and then out the door.

It bounced down the hallway and down the steps.

It bounced off Ricky Pepper's head.

And onto Lacey the cat's tail.

Then the ball careened high into the air, where it just missed clobbering Elvis the lovebird.

Finally, the froosbetball hit the single worst possible thing in the universe: Sal's treasured trophy . . .

Which was knocked off the mantel and onto the floor, where it smashed into bits.

The Peppers all gasped at once.

Sal slowly walked over to his ruined prize. His mouth kept opening like he was trying to speak, but nothing came out.

No Pepper moved.

No Pepper breathed.

Except for Megs Pepper, who bounded heavily down the stairs. "Okay, guys! Let's get this show on the road! I'm ready to go meet Centaura!" Then she noticed her siblings'

WHAM!
Oof!
BAM!
MEOW!
WHEW!
MISS!
CRACK

fear-filled eyes. "Hey, why does everyone look as though someone died?"

Sal's cheeks colored flame red. His hair stood on end. And when he pointed, his finger shook with rage.

CHAPTER 3

All the Peppers loaded into Sal's food truck, the Chili Chikka-Wow-Wow, to drive over to the convention.

All the Peppers except for one, that is.

The punishment for breaking Sal's prized possession was harsh. There would be no Comic Con for Megs this year.

She had pleaded with her father. She had cried. Her mother and brothers and sisters had begged Sal to change his mind. They all knew how important meeting Centaura was to Megs.

Yet Sal wouldn't budge. "It's a Pepper rule: Trash a trophy, take a time-out!"

But he didn't understand that this was a once-in-a-lifetime chance for Megs. Centaura had never come to San Pimento before and might never again. Megs might NEVER get to meet her! The thought of it sent her into a fresh bout of sobs as she watched the food truck disappear over a hill.

Megs reached for something to blow her nose on and accidentally used one of her favorite Centaura comic books.

She looked down at the slightly snotty cover. In this issue, Commander Cranium had discovered Centaura's only weakness: Sugar cubes from her native island of Equinia made her powerless. The only chance she had to stop the Commander was by pretending to be some other hero . . . one he wouldn't think to use the sugar cubes against! Luckily, her pal Iron Maiden was in town and let her borrow her super suit and lightning guitar. Cranium

HA HA HA! THESE SUGAR CUBES FROM CENTAURA'S ISLAND OF EQUINIA SAP HER POWER ALTOGETHER.
I'M POWERLESS! WHAT WILL I DO?
WELL, CENTAURA, I'D GIVE YOU THE ARMOR OFF MY BACK IF IT WOULD HELP.
WHY ARE YOU LOOKING AT ME SO FUNNY?
THANK GOODNESS IRON MAIDEN LOANED ME HER SUIT! COMMANDER CRANIUM HAS NO IDEA IT'S REALLY ME!
BAH! THESE CUBES WON'T WORK AGAINST IRON MAIDEN! WHAT GOOD ARE THEY EVEN???
THROW AWAY!

thought he was fighting someone else entirely!

This gave Megs a crazy idea.

Maybe *Megs Pepper* was forbidden from attending Comic Con, but if she could come up with a clever enough disguise, her family would never know it was her, even if they bumped into her!

Megs didn't have a costume ready, so she would have to improvise.

First things first: Her purple hair was a dead giveaway.

She borrowed a wig Beta had used in one of his vampire movies. Instantly, her hair went from perfectly purple to riotously red!

Next she swiped a pair of

red rubber gloves from the kitchen and a belt from her softball uniform, which she paired with her mom's yellow yoga outfit and a pair of old shorts. Then she cut some eyeholes out of one of Meemaw's sleeping masks. Using red felt from the crafts table, Megs stitched a large *F* onto the chest. Finally, a red bath towel tied around her neck made a perfect cape.

She admired herself in the mirror.

In a heroic voice she said, "This isn't a job for Megs Pepper. This is a job for . . . *Fan Girl*!"

FAN GiRL!
F

Then she leapt down the front steps of the house and bounded off to take a city bus to the convention center.

Next stop: Comic Con!!!

CHAPTER 4

The convention was everything Megs dreamt it would be and more!

Aisle after aisle held new delights to look at. Every comic, every movie, every video game seemed to have its very own booth!

And then there were the hundreds of adults

and kids who, like Megs, had dressed up as superheroes, aliens, and video game characters. It was totally awesome! And no one looked twice at her. Her costume was perfect.

There were a million things she wanted to look at, but she had to focus on her mission. Megs needed to find Centaura and get home

before her family did. Bonus points if she could avoid running into any of them . . .

She looked up and saw a video screen overhead that showed Centaura in action! Megs's jaw fell open as she watched Centaura hold up her uni-horn and say, "By the power of Equinia . . ." And then with a blinding flash of light, she became a centaur and trampled bad guys with her hooves. Words scrolled across the screen: TODAY AT COMIC CON, THE SENSATIONAL CENTAURA!

As Megs inched back to get a better look, she stepped on someone's foot. A familiar voice growled, "Hey, watch it!" She turned to find her big brother, Ricky, and instantly froze.

"Miss, do you mind? You're kinda blocking our photo!"

Megs realized that Ricky was posing for a photo with a bunch of the Defenders of Justice Club fans, and she was standing between them and the photographer.

Amazingly, Ricky didn't seem to recognize her at all!

"Sorry! I'll move," she mumbled.

"Wait! I didn't mean to be rude. I really like your costume. Are you . . . Fight Girl?"

Megs shook her head.

A teenager dressed as the Underwaterer,

King of Atlantis, asked, "Are you Phantom Girl?"

"Well, 'phantom' isn't spelled with an *F*, it just sounds like it is. Actually, I call myself . . ."

Before she could finish, the photographer cried, "Say cheese!"

As soon as the camera flashed, Megs ran and hid behind a huge replica of a time-traveling port-o-potty from the *Doctor Why* TV show.

That was a close one!

She turned a corner into the fantasy section and suddenly, *WHAM!* She ran into someone hard. She backed away as the tall figure in a long pink cloak turned dramatically to reveal . . . her mother, Tee, talking to a group of *Game of Musical Chairs* fans!

Megs could not believe her bad luck.

One of the fans rumbled at Megs, "What ho! How dare you touch the royal person of

NOT
A REAL
DRAGON.
NOT
A REAL
ZOMBIE.
NOT
A REAL
SWORD.
NOT
A REAL
AX.
BUMP!

Queen Celery!" He looked her up and down. "Hey, who are you supposed to be, anyway? Fire Woman?"

"No."

"Phlegm Lass?"

"Well, 'phlegm' isn't spelled with an *F*. Actually, I call myself . . ."

Tee interrupted them. "Enough! Let us hasten to Event Room C, where they are previewing the newest season of *Game of Musical Chairs*. Child, I dismiss thee!"

Megs didn't have to be told twice. She curtsied awkwardly and backed away quickly down the aisle in the direction she'd come from.

Tee and the other fans hurried off to the screening.

Megs breathed a sigh of relief. However, no sooner had she escaped her mom than she was hit in the head with something soft. And then again! She caught the third whatever-it-was, and examined it. It was a stuffed alien Trooble doll from the television show *Star Trucks.*

Megs wheeled around to see Scoochy standing on a table full of *Star Trucks* toys and books. Her little sister was winding up to throw another Trooble at her.

"GOT YOU, FUNNY GIRL!"

"That's Fan Girl," Megs grumbled.

"HA HA! ME CALLED BAD BABY! BAD BABY GO DO MORE BAD STUFF!" Scoochy lobbed the Trooble at Megs, who easily dodged it. Then the toddler leapt off the table and ran off to catch up to her mother, cackling all the way.

Well, at least Megs was sure her disguise worked.

Still, she needed to find Centaura and get out of there quickly. Comic Con was crawling with Peppers!

Megs looked at her map, found the booth where Centaura was appearing, and took off to meet her hero . . .

A big, burly security guard monitored the line to meet Centaura. Megs ran up to him breathlessly.

"You gotta have a ticket to be in this line," he said in a way that made it clear if you didn't have a ticket, there was zero chance you would be meeting Centaura.

Megs smiled and held up her ticket proudly. "I have a ticket! A *special* one!"

"Good for you. The *special* ticket line starts way over there . . ."

Megs turned and instantly slumped. The line to meet Centaura stretched all the way down the aisle and around the corner.

She walked what felt like a mile to the back of the line.

She took her place behind a very talkative young man.

"Have you met Centaura before?" he asked.

"No, and with this line I may never," Megs muttered.

"Well, *I* have. *I've* met her twenty times! We're practically *BFFs* at this point. That means *best fans forever*! Ha! I'm getting her to sign this giant hardcover Centaura book."

Twenty times?!? Megs would be happy to meet Centaura just once.

Her neighbor, who introduced himself as Lenny, kept bothering her with questions as they waited. "So what are you supposed to be, anyway? Furious Girl? You sound a little grumpy."

"No."

"Oh, I know! Phoenix Woman!"

"Phoenix doesn't start with an *F.* Actually, I'm calling myself . . ."

Suddenly, a cry echoed across the convention center. "Stop that thief! He stole my purse!"

Both Megs and Lenny turned to see a man in a black mask running down the aisle toward them. He was indeed carrying a purse.

The thief zipped past all sorts of caped superheroes and intergalactic champions. Except these were all just regular people in costume and not actual heroes at all. They stared

RARE COMIX
HEROES
FIGHTIN' CRIME!

in frozen shock as he passed. The only person who chased the hoodlum was the giant, muscled security guard, and all that muscle slowed him down.

Megs turned to Lenny. "Can I borrow your book?"

"Uh, sure?"

"Thanks!"

In one move she grabbed the book from Lenny and swung it out into the aisle like a baseball bat.

SMACK! The thief in the ski mask collided

with the book like it was a brick wall. He wobbled in the air for a bit and then slumped to the ground in a moaning heap.

The big guard arrived, huffing and puffing, and grabbed the woozy criminal.

Megs picked up the purse. It was purple with a big, bejeweled *C* on it.

A voice behind her said, "Ahem, do you mind if I get that back, citizen?"

Megs knew that voice like she knew her own. "Cen . . . Cen . . . Cen . . ."

Lenny squealed, "Centaura! Centaura! It's me!!! Lenny!

Remember? I've been at *all* your signings! Will you sign my book?" He snatched the book back from Megs and held it out to Centaura.

"Sure thing, friend." She quickly scribbled in the book and handed it back to Lenny. Then she turned to Megs and smiled. "I was just about to take my lunch break. The least I can do for the superhero who just saved me is buy her lunch. What do you say?"

Centaura flashed Megs a charming smile.

At first Megs turned around to make sure that Centaura wasn't talking to someone else. But everyone in line was staring with wide eyes at *her*. Megs couldn't believe it. This was really happening . . . Her favorite hero wanted to buy her lunch! "Wow, that would be amazing," she answered.

As the pair strode off together, Lenny looked

closely at Centaura's signature in his book. "Hey! You signed this to Larry! Who's Larry?"

He shook his head sadly, unaware of the excited girl with the digital camera standing nearby.

Annie Pepper pressed the stop button. She had recorded the entire incident. "Oh boy, a mysterious new superhero just saved Centaura, and I got it all!" she exclaimed. "This is going to be a huge story on SPN News!"

CHAPTER 6

In the convention center's cafeteria, Megs and Centaura ordered burgers and fries and found a table. Centaura's arrival caused quite a commotion. People stared at her and whispered excitedly. Megs noticed that the world-famous superhero wasn't simply comfortable with all the attention; she seemed to really like it. Centaura even smiled happily for photos. Megs basked in the glow of her idol while chowing down on the best burger she could remember eating in her life. She peppered her hero with questions between bites.

"So, do you have your uni-horn of power on you?"

"Er, no. I left it back at my Temple of Time-Out," Centaura replied. ". . . to keep it safe!"

"How about your coat of invisibility?"

"That, too," Centaura said quickly,

then changed the subject. "So, what's your superhero name, anyway?"

"I call myself Fan Girl," Megs said.

"Nice! And you fight crime?"

Megs thought about this for a moment. She'd only been in the superhero game for a few hours now and had already foiled a crime. "Geez. I guess so!"

Centaura nodded. "Well, you're doing a great job. I mean, that was really brave, the way you totally took out that thief." She added under her breath, "Really, really brave!"

Megs said, "Are you kidding me? I've seen you fight twenty bad guys at the same time!"

"Well, sure, another minute and I would have trampled that troublemaker!" said Centaura. "I meant, it was brave for someone who *doesn't* have my amazing superpowers!"

She thought for a moment as she chewed on a fry. "I have an idea, Fan Girl. I'll be in San Pimento for a few days. Why not team up? You could show me the town, and I could give you a couple of super pointers . . . Kind of a mentor-sidekick sort of thing. How does that sound?"

Megs gulped down the last of her hamburger and tried to speak. "Uh . . . YEAH. That sounds amazing. Unbelievable, really."

She wanted to ask a million questions, but just then she glanced at the clock and remembered she had to run. She really needed to be home before her mom and dad!

"Can we start tomorrow?" she asked. "I have a really important super mission to attend to!"

Centaura smiled and ran a hand through her awesome purple hair. "Sure, Fan Girl.

Tomorrow's fine. I should probably get back to my booth before that line turns into an angry mob, anyway. Let's meet here at noon, okay?"

"Okay!" agreed Megs as she headed for the door. "And thanks for the hamburger, Centaura!"

Centaura called after her, "It's the least I could do for the fantastic Fan Girl!"

Megs made it home before the rest of her family, but only just barely. She ran up to her room, tore off her Fan Girl costume and wig, and quickly stuffed them in her backpack.

Then she lay down on her bed and stared up at her Centaura posters. There was still a blank spot there with the purple paint poking through, but that didn't matter anymore, because Megs had something ten million times better. She had an invitation to be Centaura's sidekick and show her around San Pimento tomorrow! She couldn't wait.

The familiar rumble of the Chili Chikka-Wow-Wow drifted through the window, signaling that her family was home.

A few minutes later, there was a soft knock on her bedroom door.

"Come in," she said, trying to sound as sad as she would have been if she had actually missed the convention. She sighed heavily to really sell it.

Her father, Sal, tiptoed in.

"Pumpkin?" He sounded really, *really* guilty as he sat on the edge of her bed. "Listen, I know you didn't mean to break the trophy. It was an accident . . ."

Tee poked her head through the door. She was still dressed like Queen Celery. "Tell her! Your queen commands you!" she ordered dramatically.

Sal nodded. "Well, we feel bad . . ."

"We?" hissed Tee.

"I! *I* feel bad that I grounded you from Comic Con, and so I asked Annie . . ."

"I?" hissed Tee.

"We! *We* asked Annie to stand in line for you, and, well . . ." Sal pulled out a rolled-up tube of paper. He unfurled it. It was a poster of Centaura, and it was signed "To Megs."

Megs felt a twinge of guilt at her own dishonesty.

She gave Sal a big hug. “Thanks, Dad. I’m super sorry about breaking your trophy.”

“Pfft.” He waved her off. “I’ll just have to win the trophy for Best Chili next year.” He smacked his lips. “All this talk of chili sure is making me hungry! How about a big bowl of my newest recipe: Super Bean Chili?"

"How are the beans super?" asked Megs.

"The last time I ate a bowl of them, they made me super tooty!"

They both laughed.

Downstairs at the kitchen table, all of her brothers and sisters were crowded around their mom's laptop, pushing one another out of the way to get a better look at the screen.

"ME WANT SEE! ME WANT SEE!" Scoochy roared, pulling on Annie's ponytail.

"Owww! Okay! Okay!"

Megs asked, "Hey, guys, what's up?"

Ricky turned to her, his cheeks flushed. "Some cool new superhero at Comic Con stopped a thief who had snatched Centaura's purse!"

Megs pushed her brothers and sisters aside

to reach the computer. It was true. Someone had filmed Megs stopping the thief. The video was posted on the San Pimento Network News website. She looked at how many people had viewed it. Over five thousand??? How was that even possible? It had happened just a few hours ago! After Megs and Centaura walked away, the camera turned around to show that it was Annie who had been filming.

She spoke into the camera in her reporter voice. "Who is this mystery woman in yellow? Is she San Pimento's newest hero? What does the *F* stand for, anyway? Photogenic Woman? No, of course not. That word only sounds like it starts with an *F*! San Pimento's intrepid reporter, Annie Pepper, is on the case and plans to find out more . . . after I get a signed Centaura poster for my sister."

The video ended, and everyone turned to Annie, who nodded proudly. "Yep, I got it all on film! This new superhero is the scoop of the century!"

"Good. We need more female superheroes," said their mother. "The only woman in the Defenders of Justice Club is that sidekick of Private Patriot . . . What was her name again?"

"Plucky," answered Ricky. "But she's fictional.

This superhero . . . whoever she is . . . she's totally for real. And she's AMAZING!"

Maria asked, "Hmm. I wonder if she has an agent?"

"SCOOCHY NOT BAD BABY! NO! NO! SCOOCHY NOW GOOD BABY!" screeched the toddler, tearing off her supervillain costume dramatically. Everyone thought that she might have another costume underneath, but it was just a really naked Scoochy.

"Super Bean Chili's up!" cried Sal happily, ladling bowlfuls of chili for the whole family.

Megs had a sinking feeling that all this attention might just land her in trouble. Suddenly she wasn't super hungry for chili after all.

The next day, Megs snuck out to meet Centaura. She carefully hid her Fan Girl outfit in her backpack so that none of her brothers or sisters would discover her secret. Then, later, she changed in the stall of the convention center bathroom.

Her hero was right where she said she would be.

"Hi, Centaura!" said Megs. "Here I am! What would you like to do today? Fight some crime? Maybe use your uni-horn of power to foil an evil plot to take over the world? Oh right, I forgot you had to leave it in your Temple of Time-Out. Oh, I know! How about some super intense sidekick combat training!" Megs imitated a couple of martial arts moves she'd seen Centaura use in her movies.

Centaura considered this. "Hmmm, all good ideas. But before we can fight crime, we need the right equipment. I love your costume, Fan Girl, but do you have anything practical? Like a grappling hook? Walkie-talkies? A fanny pack, at least?"

Megs shook her head sadly. She didn't have any of that stuff!

"Well, I think this calls for a visit to the mall!"

The San Pimento Mall sat right next to the convention center. Floor after floor of stores rose up above them.

As they strolled through the complex, Megs noticed more people gawking at Centaura. Now they were whispering and smiling toward Megs as well. She assumed at least some of them had seen yesterday's video on the internet. Centaura just smiled and waved. It all made Megs a little uncomfortable. She wondered if it wouldn't have been smarter to walk around as Megs Pepper and Delores Duchess instead. They would get a lot less attention that way.

After some exploring, Centaura found the perfect store. It was called The Sharper Hero. Centaura looked approvingly in the window. "Ah, here's the stuff: Belts! Cables! Oooh, capes! I always wanted a cape! And I see they have them in purple!"

Centaura strode in like she owned the place. A number of salespeople came running over

and surrounded her, showing her gadgets, gizmos, and all sorts of useful gear.

Megs hovered in the doorway. She was about to join Centaura when she heard a faint cry.

"Help! Help!"

Megs tried to get her hero's attention. "Centaura! Do you hear that? Someone's calling for help!"

But Centaura was twirling in a purple cape in front of a mirror, with salespeople fawning over her.

Again Megs heard the shouting voice, which sounded more frantic than ever. "Help! My baby!"

Baby??? thought Megs. She couldn't spare a second more, and ran out of the store toward the cries for help.

At last she came to a crowd of people

standing outside a store called Big Bobby's Balloonarama. A mother was pointing toward the ceiling and crying hysterically, "My baby! My baby! Someone help my baby!"

That isn't just any mother, Megs thought. *It's my mother!* That meant the baby must be . . . Megs gasped and followed Tee's trembling finger upward.

Indeed, her little sister Scoochy was floating high above the crowd, holding on to a gigantic balloon that was slowly making its way toward the mall's glass ceiling.

Scoochy screamed happily, "ME SUPERHERO! ME FLY!"

The owner of the store, Big Bobby, was frantic, too. "That balloon was a display item only! It clearly said DO NOT TOUCH! Geez Louise!"

MY BABY!
BIG BOBBY'S BALLOONARAMA

Megs could see that the balloon was heading right for a flagpole that had a very pointy end. One touch and, pop, Scoochy would fall! Megs was sure that a fall like that could seriously hurt her sister . . . or worse!

There wasn't a moment to spare. Megs looked around frantically for something she could use to save Scoochy.

There was a coffee shop called The Caffeine Bean. No.

Yo-Yo Yogurt? Megs didn't think there was time to make a soft serve big enough to catch a kid.

"AHA!" Megs shouted as she spotted Trampoline Town. A gigantic trampoline sat right outside the store.

She tried to push it, but it was really heavy! So she called out to a few people watching the floating toddler in terror. “Please! Help me with this!”

Then, working as a team, Megs and the bystanders were able to push the trampoline right beneath Scoochy.

But Megs wasn’t done. She climbed up on the trampoline and started bouncing. She had taken loads of gymnastic classes. She loved the beams and the floor routines, but her favorite moments were always on the trampoline—it

was the closest thing to flying that she had ever experienced.

If only she could fly now! Or turn into a leaping centaur like Centaura!

Keeping an eye on her sister, she began to bounce.

She bounced higher.

She bounced highest.

There was a tremendously loud POP as the flagpole finally poked a hole in the balloon, and suddenly Scoochy was screaming louder than a Girder City fan at the Super Bowl. And she was falling toward Megs!

Megs reached out her arms, caught her sister like a football, and then tucked and flipped. She hit the trampoline softly on her back.

As her bouncing came to a halt, she became aware of two things: that Scoochy's cries had

POP
CATCH

turned to giggles, and the gasps of the panicked crowd had turned to cheers.

She gently handed Scoochy down to Tee.

Scoochy cried, "MORE BOUNCE! MORE FLY! MORE! MORE! MORE!"

Tee said through tears of relief, "Thank you! Thank you for saving my little girl! I don't even know your name!"

Megs stood up. It was hard to look heroic when you were balancing on a wobbly trampoline, but she tried.

"You can call me Fan Girl! And we *all* saved your child!" She gestured to the crowd that had helped move the trampoline. "Remember, everyone has a hero inside them. They just have to let it out!"

Just then, Megs spotted Centaura following

the buzz of the crowd. Megs bounced off the trampoline and ran over to her.

"Centaura! Did you see? Did you see? I rescued my sis . . . I rescued a little toddler! Just like you would! Well, not 'just like,' because *you* would have turned into a centaur and used your super leap to catch her without help from anyone!"

Centaura looked stunned. "That was amazing, Fan Girl! I've never seen anything like it! You saved that little girl's life!"

Megs blushed. "I mean, it's not like the time you saved that entire busload of kids who went off the Girder City Bridge! Now that was amazing!"

Centaura shifted uncomfortably, "Well, sure, er . . ." She changed the subject quickly. "I think this calls for a celebration! How about a root beer float, partner?"

Megs felt dizzy. Did Centaura just call her "partner"? This all felt so unreal.

As they walked toward the food court, they didn't notice Annie Pepper filming everything.

She had been there the whole time, having tagged along with her mother and Scoochy. And for the second time in two days, the intrepid reporter had been in exactly the right place at exactly the right time. She couldn't believe her luck!

Annie turned the camera on herself. "Another miraculous rescue by the new superhero who has been taking San Pimento by storm . . . Fan Girl!"

Scoochy tried to grab the camera from her sister's hands. "FAN GIRL SAVE SCOOCHY! FAN GIRL SAVE SCOOCHY!"

“Cut it out, Scooch!” Annie swatted her sister away and smiled at the camera. “But who is Fan Girl? Where does she come from, and what does she want? Annie Pepper aims to find out!”

After celebrating the amazing rescue, Centaura said she had to return to her hotel to take some meetings about her next movie, and then she had to approve some Centaura T-shirt designs, but they could meet again tomorrow if Megs liked.

Megs jumped at the chance!

At home the family was again buzzing. This time Annie’s footage of Fan Girl coming to the rescue was the biggest story on the San Pimento Network News! The whole Pepper family had crowded around the television to watch the report.

Megs walked in just in time to hear the anchorman say, "Welcome to SPN News. In tonight's top story, one of our reporters, Annie Pepper, has sent in some fantastic footage she filmed earlier today at the San Pimento Mall, where America's newest superhero, Fan Girl, rescued a toddler from certain balloon doom! Let's watch!"

The Peppers oohed and aahed as they watched Fan Girl push over the trampoline and then catch the falling Scoochy. Megs had to admit, she looked pretty impressive. She oohed and aahed right along with them. And she made double sure that her costume was zipped away safely in her backpack where no one could see it!

The report ended with a great close-up of Fan Girl saying, "Remember, everyone has a hero in them. They just have to let it out!"

The family turned off the television and applauded.

"Great job, Annie!" said Meemaw.

Tee wiped sweat off her brow. "Just watching that stresses me out. Thank goodness Fan Girl was there!"

Maria chimed in. "Fan Girl? FAN GIRL??? Are you kidding me? That's an *awful* name. She needs a rebranding . . . more importantly, she needs an *agent*."

"Well, I think she's super cool," Ricky announced. "Right, Beta?" Ricky tried to nudge Beta in the side, but his elbow passed right through his brother like a ghost. "Huh?"

Beta, who had been playing a new video game during the broadcast, looked up. "Oh, sorry, guys, I'm playing Uplayit Virtual Reality

in my bedroom. I'm not actually here. This is just a hologram!"

Meanwhile, Scoochy had written a big backward *S* on her belly using a marker. She was running around the living room trying to "save" their pets. This basically meant grabbing them and squeezing the life out of them.

She shrieked, "SCOOCHY NOW SUPER! SCOOCHY RESCUE YOU!"

Megs couldn't believe it. She was totally getting away with it. The Peppers didn't know their new idol's secret identity, but they definitely had Fan Girl fever!

CHAPTER 8

The next day Megs met her new BFF on the boardwalk. Sal gave her a ride. He was setting up his food truck at the beach that day.

Once he'd found a good spot, Megs hopped out of the Chili Chikka-Wow-Wow truck, waved goodbye to her dad, and ducked into the public restroom to change into her Fan Girl costume.

When she emerged, a few people pointed at her and said, "Look! It's Fan Girl!"

Wow, she thought. *It must be so cool to get that sort of reaction everywhere you go!* She couldn't believe that Centaura had it happen every day (times one hundred).

She found her new costumed friend at the boardwalk gazebo, where they had agreed to meet.

The superhero pair strolled down the boardwalk. Centaura got them ice cream cones. Megs got a scoop of chocolatly-chocolate with chocolate syrup, and Centaura got a super pink everyberry cone with rainbow sprinkles.

"So what's on the agenda today?" Megs asked. "I know you took it easy on me

yesterday because it was my first day, but I think I proved that I've got the makings of a great sidekick! Let's go fight some crime! Let's do some superheroing!" She picked up a piece of litter and tossed it dramatically into a trash can. "Look! I just superheroed some litter. Fan Girl to the rescue!"

Centaura fixed her hair in a storefront reflection. "Honestly, Fan Girl, I'm a little tired today. I was up super late working on my new memoir, *No Horsing Around: The Centaura*

Story. I was hoping we could just do a little relaxing—maybe play some Skee-Ball, ride the roller coaster. This boardwalk has an arcade, and cotton candy . . ." She looked around and pointed. "There's someone that draws portraits of you while you wait! Doesn't that sound fun? I love having my portrait drawn!"

They walked over to the caricaturist.

Megs had an idea. "Hey, what if you change into your horse form for this? I bet it would make the picture extra cool!"

Centaura shook her head sadly. "You know my centaur powers can only be used in the biggest emergencies, Fan Girl."

Megs sighed. So far the day wasn't nearly as exciting as she'd hoped it would be.

The pair sat for the portrait artist. They were supposed to hold still, and Centaura sat like a statue, mid-wink and smiling. But after about five minutes, Megs began tapping her foot impatiently. She loved hanging out with Centaura, but she was bored.

Just then, Megs heard a commotion coming from down the boardwalk.

She craned her neck to get a look, but the crowd that was gathering was too far away.

The portrait artist reminded her to keep still.

"I think something fishy is going on over there," Megs said through smiling teeth. "We'd better investigate!"

"Now, now, Fan Girl," Centaura scolded. "Investigating strange commotions may be important, but isn't respecting this man's time and business important as well?"

The artist smiled. "Beautiful words! And your profile isn't too shabby, either!"

Megs rolled her eyes. "Fine."

But the hubbub continued. Megs thought she heard a faint whimpering and the snap of a whip. She couldn't stay still any longer.

"Sorry, Centaura, Mr. Artist . . . I think someone needs my help!"

Megs stood up and ran off down the boardwalk toward the noise.

The painter shook his head. "The nerve! I'll make this one a solo portrait!" He started erasing Fan Girl from the canvas.

As Megs reached the source of the commotion, she found the snarling carnival manager standing angrily over a mangy old mutt, who was cowering against the walled entrance to the boardwalk carnival rides.

"Bad dog!" the manager roared. "Bad dog!" He snapped his belt at the dog, and it cracked like a whip.

Behind the manager stood a woman with her arm around a boy who seemed to be nursing a bite on his hand.

"That dog bit my Timmy!" She sniffed. "He's a nuisance and should be put down immediately! He might have rabies!"

People on the boardwalk had stopped to watch.

The manager snarled. "No one bites my customers and gets away with it!"

The dog cowered as the man started toward him.

But Fan Girl leapt between him and the dog. She held up her hand for the manager to stop!

"What's going on here?" she demanded.

The woman pointed an accusing finger at the dog. "That dog bit my sweet angel here!"

Megs looked at Timmy. She knew Timmy from school. He was no angel. In fact, he was a bit of a bully.

"Timmy, can I see where the dog bit you?" Megs asked calmly.

Timmy held his hand out. Megs couldn't see a bite mark. But she did see some greenish sticky residue on his hand.

Suspicious, Megs thought. "Timmy, did you do anything to the dog to make it try to bite you?"

"No! It just leapt out at me and tried to kill me! For no reason at all!"

Megs looked down at the dog. The poor thing looked sad and hungry. You could actually see its ribs sticking out through its patchy coat. And it definitely needed a bath. Then Megs saw something interesting: A green lollipop had stuck itself to the dog's side. She pulled it gently off the dog and patted the mutt on the head. It cowered at her touch.

"This dog is clearly too scared to hurt anyone!" She pointed the lollipop at Timmy.

"When he attacked you, were you by any chance poking him with this green lollipop?"

"Uh, no! I've never even seen that lollipop," Timmy lied.

"Oh no? Well, if you weren't eating a green lollipop, then why don't you stick out your tongue for all of us to see?"

Timmy realized his mistake, but too late. The crowd loomed over him, as did the carnival manager. Even his mother had leaned in close.

Slowly, he stuck out his tongue, hoping that it wouldn't be lime green.

But it was.

Timmy's tongue was so green that it practically glowed.

Megs pointed at it gleefully. "Ha! So you *were* teasing the dog with the lollipop!"

It was true. Timmy had just come from the candy store and had been tormenting the hungry dog.

"Well, maybe I was teasing him a little! But it was just a couple of pokes!"

"Out of the way, girl!" roared the carnival manager, who still clearly wanted to get rid of the stray.

But Megs stood her ground. In fact, she stood extra tall.

"That's *Fan* Girl! And you'll have to go through me to get to the dog!"

"Fine by me!" roared the manager. He tried to push his way past Megs, but the entire crowd of onlookers rushed between the two of them.

"Don't you lay a finger on her!" threatened a man wearing roller skates.

"Yeah, leave her alone!" said a frizzy-haired jogger.

Musicians who'd been busking in a two-person horse costume spoke up next. "You touch her, you gotta go through me first," said the person in the horse's head.

"And I'll be right behind him—literally!" That came from the horse's butt.

The carnival manager was big and mean, but he was no dummy. "Hey, uh, listen, this was just a misunderstanding! That lady could sue me!"

Megs glanced at Timmy's mother, who now looked very uncomfortable.

"You're not going to sue anyone, are you, ma'am?"

"Oh, it probably isn't worth it . . ." The woman quickly grabbed Timmy's hand and pulled him away. Timmy stuck his green tongue out at Megs as they rushed off.

"Great job, Fan Girl! Well done!" the crowd

cheered, just as Centaura came running up.

"Fan Girl! Are you all right?" she asked breathlessly.

Megs patted the poor, mistreated dog. "I'm fine, but this guy almost wasn't. Thankfully all these kind people helped." The crowd had grown more excited now that Centaura had shown up. They were taking photos with her, shaking her hand, and the roller skater even asked her to sign his helmet. Centaura for once looked as though she didn't want all the attention.

When the crowd began to disperse, Megs said a bit tersely, "I can't believe you didn't come and help!"

Centaura gestured back at the artist. "I told you. I couldn't just leave him. He was in the middle of drawing my portrait!"

Megs sighed. "Sometimes one thing is more important than the other. Like right now, the most important thing is to get this poor little pup over to Frida Flamingo's Animal Adoption Agency. It needs a bath and some food." She picked up the dog and cradled it in her arms. "Are you going to come?"

Centaura seemed very uncomfortable and a bit embarrassed. "I would, but I have another important call with my agent in a half hour . . . so . . ."

"Sure, sure. I get it," Megs said as she turned and headed down the boardwalk. "See you around, Centaura."

Centaura watched her go,

then her proud shoulders slumped and she walked off the other way.

Annie Pepper stepped out of the thinning crowd with her camera.

"Another daring rescue by San Pimento's newest hero, Fan Girl! How does she end up in just the right place when she's needed? And more importantly, how do I always end up right there to record it on my camera?"

Someone poked Annie in the shoulder.

She turned around and saw a masked man in a costume with a big *P* emblazoned on his shirt.

He smiled at Annie. "Those are two very good questions that I'd like to get an answer to!"

"Who are you?" asked Annie.

"I'm San Pimento's newest villain, *the Poker*!" He let out a crazy laugh.

"And what's your power?"

"Isn't it obvious? I poke people! I've decided it's the only way I can get anyone's attention. First I'll poke you, and then I'll poke my greatest nemesis . . . Centaura! And then everyone will remember me!"

With another crazy laugh, he held up a gloved finger. "Pokey-bye-baby!" he shouted as purple smoke hissed out of the glove's finger.

Annie coughed, and then she fell asleep.

CHAPTER 9

At home, the Peppers crowded around the television to watch a special news report. But this time none of the Peppers looked happy about it. That's because this time Annie was tied up! In fact, she was tied to the pointing finger on a giant robotic hand, and it was pointed right at the convention center!

NYAH HA HA!
CONVENTION CENTER
CONVENTIONS

"This is Annie Pepper, reporting live. I am being held hostage by a supervillain who calls himself the Poker! And he has a message for Centaura."

"Hey-o, San Pimento. My name's the Poker. And boy do I love poking things! It really gets people's attention. Today, I'm going to give the convention center a poke so big there won't be a place for Comic Con next year. And maybe then you'll all remember the greatest supervillain San Pimento has ever seen! Unless, of course, Miss Oh-So-Popular Centaura shows up. Then we can see if my Power Poker can beat her centaur hooves! My giant robotic poking machine is going to wipe the floor with her! Nyah ha ha ha!!!" The Poker laughed and danced and clapped like a crazy person.

Annie struggled against her restraints and

pleaded at the camera. "Please, Centaura and Fan Girl! Please rescue me! You're my only hope!"

The Poker lunged in front of her. "Oh, and remember, that's *the Poker*. Spelled P-O-K—" The transmission cut off abruptly before he could finish spelling his name.

The Peppers looked at one another.

"Annie's in trouble!" cried Sal. "I sure hope Centaura or Fan Girl gets there soon!"

Tee shook her head. "That's our little girl out there! We can't wait for superheroes! We have to try to rescue her on our own," said Tee decisively.

"But how?" Sal cried. "We're just regular people! We're not super!!!"

"Has anyone seen Megs? She's been gone all day," added Ricky suspiciously.

Scoochy roared and pointed to the *S* on her chest. "ME SUPER! ME SUPER!"

Maria thought for a moment. "Remember when Fan Girl saved Scoochy? What was it she said?" She snapped her fingers. "I've got it! 'Remember, everyone has a hero in them . . . They just have to let it out!'" She smiled. "Peppers, I may just have come up with a plan!"

An hour later, the Poker paced and checked his watch again. "What is keeping Centaura?"

"She'll be here . . . I hope," said Annie.

The Poker shook his head. "She's always rescuing kids with balloons and stray dogs, but you try to destroy a huge building with a giant Power Poker, and suddenly she can't be bothered?"

Annie corrected him. "I'm pretty sure Fan Girl did those things, not Centaura."

"Well, sure, but Centaura was there!"

"Yet she didn't actually *do* anything."

The Poker poked his chin. "I hadn't really thought about that."

Suddenly a blob of chili smacked him in the cheek.

The Poker snarled angrily. "Who dares to deface my . . . face?"

A group of voices called out, "We do!"

The Poker turned to find a bunch of superheroes he didn't recognize running toward him. "Who in the blue blazes are you people???"

"I'm Chili Dude! I can sling chili with deadly aim!" Sal wore a big *C* and carried a bucket of his Super Spicy Chili. He ladled another glob at the Poker.

"Hey!" said the Poker. "That's hot!"

Tee had added a pink mask to her Queen Celery costume. "I'm Queen Tee! No one disobeys my commands!"

Ricky had put on his Private Patriot costume, but had also stapled a big *R* to his chest. "I'm the Rad Crusher! I have the power to crush *on* anything!" Ricky hoped that the Poker didn't catch that "on" part. He'd really tried to play it down.

Behind Ricky, five identical Betas punched the air. "Call me Max Man! I can make copies of myself!" He'd used Uplayit Virtual Reality to create lots of holograms of himself, but the Poker didn't know that!

Maria, in a business suit and a mask, said, "I'm Super Agent! I have an aggressive personality and I'm not afraid to take ten percent out of you!"

Scoochy ran at the Poker as fast as her legs could toddle. She was completely naked except for a mask fashioned from a diaper she'd put on

CONTRACTS!
CENSORED

her head and a big backward *S* on her chest. "ME MEAN STREAK! ME DESTROY YOU!!!!" Nudity wasn't really a power, but Scoochy made up for it with enthusiasm.

When the whole family had assembled, each member stood tall and cried out, "Together, we are the Super Peppers!"

The Poker wasn't impressed. "You guys look like a bunch of Comic Con clowns and rejects. Prepare to be poked!"

He typed "SCOOP" into the remote control that controlled the Power Poker. The giant robotic hand turned, opened, and scooped the family right up. Then it returned to poking position and swiveled back toward the convention center, ready to poke the building to rubble.

Peppers stuck out of the clenched fist in all

sorts of weird ways. But the robotic fingers held them tightly.

The Poker just laughed. "No more nobodies! I want the super battle of the century! Centaura, where are you???"

CHAPTER 10

Delores Duchess sat on her hotel bed in her bathrobe and watched the news in horror. That madman looked really scary and dangerous. She hoped the police would show up soon to stop him!

There was a knock on the door.

Room service, she thought. *Finally!* She'd ordered it ages ago! Nothing made her hungrier than actual, real-life danger.

She opened the door and was shocked to see Fan Girl standing there.

Fan Girl did not look happy.

"Are you back from dropping off that stray dog so soon?" Delores asked. "I was just about to take an important call from Hollywood . . . Maybe you should come back later!"

She smiled apologetically and tried to shut the door, but Megs blocked it with her foot. Delores took a few surprised steps backward.

"You're not the Centaura I thought you

were!" Megs said as she stormed into the hotel room. "How come you're not down at the convention center fighting the Poker? I thought you were a superhero! I thought we were friends!"

"I can't." Delores looked down at the floor.

Megs pointed angrily at the television set. Ricky seemed squished, Maria looked green, and Beta shivered in fear. Then she pulled off her mask and wig and started to cry. "I'm not really a superhero! I don't have any superpowers! The Poker is going to hurt my family, and I can't help them. But you can! You have actual superpowers!"

Delores Duchess flopped on the bed. "No, Fan Girl, I don't. I don't have any powers AT ALL."

"Have Commander Cranium's sugar cubes made you powerless again?"

Delores sighed. "No, kid. I'm not really a superhero! All those movies, and comics . . . they're just make-believe!"

"But your movies look so real! And I've seen you do stuff live on television, too!"

Delores shook her head. "Those are just stunts I do to increase movie ticket sales. And I don't even do them myself. I use a stuntperson!"

"But I've seen you turn into a centaur!"

Delores slumped even lower. "That's just special effects. A film trick. I'm no hero. I'm just a big faker . . . an actor. *You're* the real hero!

I knew it when I saw you take out the purse snatcher. When you saved that baby and rescued the dog at the boardwalk. I'm just happy I get to hang out with someone as brave as you. I guess I hoped that it would rub off a little, and maybe I'd end up more like the Centaura I pretend to be to the world."

Megs couldn't believe it. "You think *I'm* brave?"

Delores nodded. "Braver than I am. Some actual supervillain wants a real fight with Centaura? How would I ever fight a giant robotic hand? I can't turn into a centaur. There's no such thing as a uni-horn of power. The Temple of Time-Out is just a fancy name I call my beach house in Malibu! Maybe Centaura would be brave enough, but not plain old Delores Duchess!" She began to cry.

"Well, I'm just plain old Megs Pepper. Believing in Centaura made me a hero." Megs passed her idol a tissue. "Maybe it's time for you to believe in yourself. I bet together we can defeat the Poker!" She put a hand out to Delores. "What do you say . . . partner?"

Delores Duchess thought for a minute and then smiled. "I guess I can't let Fan Girl fight this battle on her own. Let's go do some superheroing!"

CHAPTER 11

The Poker was tired of waiting. "If Centaura doesn't show up in the next five minutes, I'm totally going to poke down the convention center. For real!"

"Maybe she's stuck in traffic," suggested Sal Pepper.

"Rush hour in this part of town is no joke," agreed Tee.

"MEAN STREAK HUNGRY!" Scoochy tried to bite her brother Beta, but her teeth went right through him. Turns out she'd tried to bite one of the holograms.

"Maybe we should do a sit-down interview and talk about your feelings," Annie suggested to the Poker.

"I hope my hair looks okay on television," worried Ricky aloud.

"EVERYONE JUST BE QUIET!" yelled the Poker.

Just then, a voice came from above. "If you need a time-out, Poker, I'd be happy to give you one!"

Everyone looked up. Centaura stood dramatically on top of the convention center and smiled.

Her super white teeth sparkled in the sunlight. Wind blew extra dramatically through her hair.

And it wasn't just Centaura, it was Centaura in super centaur form!

The Poker clapped. "Finally! Centaura, we meet again!"

Centaura shook her head. "Sorry, Poker, but I don't think we've ever faced off."

The Poker's smile turned to a snarl. "Of course you don't remember me! Why would you? I'm nobody, and you're Miss Fancy-Hooves. Well, no one's going to forget me after I destroy the convention center!"

He pressed a number of buttons, laughing creepily, and again the Power Poker sprang to life. But this time it headed for the convention center! It was going to poke the center to smithereens, with all the Peppers in tow!

With a mighty battle cry, Centaura leapt high into the air, soaring at the robotic hand.

The Poker pushed a few more buttons and typed "POKE CENTAURA" into his remote control. The giant metallic finger swung around and shot toward Centaura.

Centaura leapt at the Power Poker.

Then, at the very last second, something truly unexpected happened.

Centaura broke into two! The top half of Centaura went one way, and the bottom half went another.

A head poked out of the back end. It was Fan Girl!

On their way over, Fan Girl and Centaura had stopped at the boardwalk and borrowed the two-person horse costume from the performers to create the illusion that Centaura was actually a centaur.

The Power Poker was programmed to attack Centaura. But it was confused. Now there were *two* Centauras to attack. Should it poke the front end? Or the rear end? It couldn't do both!

It was all too much for the poor Power Poker. The giant robotic hand started to shake, and then smoke began to rise from it. The robot made a loud *SPROING-OING-OING* sound just before a giant spring popped

out. Then the hand slumped over, completely broken.

Centaura ran over and grabbed the Poker by the scruff of his neck. "Do you give up, Poker?"

The Poker's shoulders sagged. "Yeah, I give up. I just wanted people to remember me. No one ever does!"

He took off his mask.

Fan Girl gasped.

"Larry from Comic Con?" Centaura marveled.

The Poker jumped up and down. "Lenny! My name is Lenny! I've met you twenty times and you *still* get my name wrong! I'm sorry I tried to hurt you all, but I was just so mad! I'm a person, too, you know."

Megs knew she should be angry, but instead she felt sorry for Lenny. So she decided she would try to make him feel better. She glanced

over at the Power Poker. Even though it was broken, it was still a pretty terrific invention. And suddenly, a great idea popped into her head.

"Lenny, this machine is amazing! You built it?"

Lenny sniffed and wiped his nose on his sleeve. No one had ever called Lenny "amazing" before. "Sure! I'm great with machines. I can build just about anything!"

"I was thinking . . . how hard would it be to

make a robotic horse that Centaura could ride around on?"

"Oh. That'd be easy. It would take a couple of days, though," Lenny warned them. "I used all my robotics equipment on the Power Poker. I'd have to order new parts." Police sirens could be heard in the distance. "And they probably won't let me do that sort of thing in jail."

Megs said, "Well, I bet they wouldn't send Centaura's *new sidekick* to jail. He's going to be creating all the wonderful gadgets Centaura needs to fight crime. Right, Centaura?"

Centaura looked at Lenny, and then at Megs and then back at Lenny. Realization finally dawned on her. "Ohhhh! Right, Fan Girl!"

Sal Pepper (who was still stuck in the Power Poker) piped up. "Hey, uh, can someone get us out of here?

CHAPTER 12

That night, the Peppers invited Centaura and Lenny over for a dinner of Sal's Super Spicy Chili.

Centaura had asked Lenny to become her sidekick. If he could develop gadgets that would allow her to actually become a real-life Centaura,

Delores Duchess could turn into something more important than just a Hollywood movie character. Lenny had of course accepted the offer immediately. He was already hard at work sketching a robotic horse half that would allow Centaura to become a real centaur.

"And of course, I can make you a uni-horn of power. We'll make that after we make the centaur robot!"

Centaura's mouth was too full of chili to do anything but nod. She had finished two bowlfuls already. "Wow. Actual superheroing is hungry work!" she said when she'd finished the third.

As they ate, Megs told the Peppers the whole story of her adventure.

"So you snuck out to Comic Con as Fan Girl?" Beta couldn't believe it.

Ricky yelled, "That is so cool!"

"I should ground you for that," said Sal.

"But she saved the family, so you won't," said Tee.

"But you saved the family, so I won't," Sal agreed sheepishly.

Centaura smacked her forehead. "That reminds me! I brought a thank-you gift for all your help." She reached into her glittery purse with the *C* on it and pulled out a comic safely enclosed in plastic. It was the ultra-rare copy of *Presto Pepper's Magic Comix* #1. She handed it to Meemaw with a smile. "I hear you've been looking for this for a while. But trust me, DO NOT TURN TO THE LAST PAGE!"

"Pappy's comic!" Meemaw squinted

at the cover and gave Centaura a giant toothless grin. (She'd misplaced her dentures again.)

Megs said, "I think that may have been my last adventure . . . Superheroing is super fun, but it's also super dangerous!"

Maria handed Megs a box. "Well, it may have been *Fan Girl's* last adventure, but that doesn't mean it has to be yours. And red really isn't your color."

Megs opened the box. Inside was a purple costume Maria had made especially for her.

"Fan Girl is a silly name," said Maria. "You

aren't a fan, you have fans. In fact, I see a whole table of them! I suggest Fierce Girl. And I'll take the standard ten percent as your agent!"

Everyone clapped.

Centaura said, "Fierce Girl! I love it!" She gave Megs a hug. "And I'll be president of your fan club!"

Megs blushed. She'd gotten famous, met her hero, and saved her town. Life with the Peppers really was pretty super!

The End

Can't get enough Pepper pandemonium? Look for this feisty family's first crazy catastrophe!

Annie aspires to adopt an adorable dog named Azzie. But her family fancies different furry friends. So her parents permit a parade of Pepper pet picks, and soon the siblings sink to sabotage! Who will win the clan's clash of creatures?

MEET THE PEPPERS

FUNNY RUNS IN THE FAMILY.

SCHOLASTIC

scholastic.com

PEPPERPARTY4